THE EASY
PIANO COLLECTION
GOLD

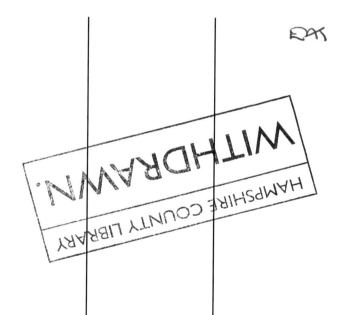

CHESTER MUSIC
part of The Music Sales Group

London/New York/Paris/Sydney/Copenhagen/Berlin/Madrid/Hong Kong/Tokyo

Published by:
Chester Music Limited,
14-15 Berners Street, London W1T 3LJ, UK.

Exclusive Distributors:
Music Sales Limited,
Distribution Centre, Newmarket Road, Bury St Edmunds, Suffolk IP33 3YB, UK.
Music Sales Corporation,
180 Madison Avenue, 24th Floor, New York NY 10010, USA.
Music Sales Pty Limited,
20 Resolution Drive, Caringbah, NSW 2229, Australia.

Order No. CH79651
ISBN 978-1-78038-629-4
This book © Copyright 2012 by Chester Music.

Compiled and Edited by Camden Music Services.
Project Manager: Ruth Power.
Cover photo courtesy of Rex Features.

CD recorded and produced by Mutual Chord Studio, Guangzhou, China.

Printed in the EU.

Your Guarantee of Quality:
As publishers, we strive to produce every book to the highest commercial standards.
The music has been freshly engraved and carefully designed to minimise
awkward page turns to make playing from it a real pleasure.
Particular care has been given to specifying acid-free, neutral-sized
paper made from pulps which have not been elemental chlorine bleached.
This pulp is from farmed sustainable forests and was produced
with special regard for the environment.
Throughout, the printing and binding have been planned to ensure a sturdy,
attractive publication which should give years of enjoyment.
If your copy fails to meet our high standards, please inform us and we will gladly replace it.
www.musicsales.com

CONTENTS/CD TRACK LISTING

The Easy Piano Collection Gold Sampler

Chester Music's best-selling series, *The Easy Piano Collection Gold*, features some of the most famous classical music composers ranging from J.S. Bach to Scott Joplin. Each of the albums highlights a particular composer's essential works, containing original piano music as well as transcriptions of other pieces. This sampler presents a selection of the finest music from the series.

Johann Sebastian Bach (1685–1750) was a giant of the Baroque era. He wrote an astonishing volume of music, both sacred and secular. Primarily a church musician, he wrote many cantatas, amongst which is the famous *Jesu, Joy Of Man's Desiring* (from Cantata 147). His secular music is full of memorable melodies, such as the second movement from his 'Orchestral Suite No.3 in D', popularly known as *Air On The G String*. *Prélude No.1 in C Major* is the first piece in Bach's '48' (two books of préludes and fugues in every key, entitled 'The Well-Tempered Clavier').

George Frideric Handel (1685–1759) was a direct contemporary of Bach. Although German by birth, he was a naturalized Englishman. His music includes some of the most popular pieces ever written. Contained in this album is the *Air* from the 'Water Music', the choral work *Zadok The Priest*, written for George II's coronation in 1727 and sung at every coronation since, and the *Sarabande in D minor*.

The balance and refinement of the Classical era is epitomized in the work of Austrian genius Wolfgang Amadeus Mozart (1756–1791). From his 'Requiem' (completed after his death by his pupil, Sussmayr) comes the *Lacrimosa*, wherein lilting rhythms depict the lamentations on judgement day. Also included is *Ave Verum Corpus*, one of Mozart's most famous works.

Ludwig van Beethoven (1770–1827) was a musical pioneer, spanning both the Classical and Romantic eras. He expanded the sonata, the symphony and the concerto, baffling and shocking audiences with his ground-breaking style, yet all the while struggling against increasing deafness. The melody in the second movement of his *Sonata Pathètique* is well-known for its beauty, and presents something of a contrast to the exciting opening of the first movement of *Symphony No.5*, which is popularly thought to depict Fate knocking at the door.

Franz Schubert's (1797–1828) gift lay in his ability to write beautiful melodies. This talent is distilled in his 600 songs (Lieder), including *Ave Maria*, and also in his chamber music such as the 'Piano Quintet in A major' known as the *Trout Quintet*.

The German Romantic composer Robert Schumann (1810–1856) wrote many pieces depicting various scenes, which he then grouped together in suites. *Träumerei* (Dreaming) is perhaps the best-known piece from 'Kinderszenen' (Scenes from Childhood).

In contrast, Polish composer Frédéric Chopin (1810–1849) did not give his pieces descriptive titles, but instead grouped them according to style, for example, waltzes, préludes, nocturnes, polonaises and mazurkas. In all, he wrote over 200 piano pieces ranging in difficulty from the virtuosic to the relatively simple. The *Nocturne in E flat* is a perfect example of Chopin's ability to spin a beautiful 'cantabile' melody over a delicate left hand accompaniment. The 24 Préludes (Op.28) were commissioned by the piano-maker and publisher Camille Pleyel. As with many of Chopin's préludes, some have been given 'nicknames', and two such préludes are included here: *Prélude in E minor 'Suffocation'* which was played at Chopin's funeral, and *Prélude in C minor 'Funeral March'* which, strangely enough, wasn't.

The works of Felix Mendelssohn (1809–1847) were Romantic in spirit, yet rooted in the Classical style. He composed a large number of short piano pieces known as 'Songs Without Words', as well as symphonies and choral works, amongst which maybe the best known is *O, For The Wings Of A Dove* from the cantata 'Hear My Prayer'.

The Russian Romantic, Pyotr Ilyich Tchaikovsky (1840–1893), was a great orchestral composer, remembered particularly for his three ballet scores, 'Swan Lake', 'The Sleeping Beauty' and 'The Nutcracker'. Presented here are transcriptions of the rousing *March Of The Toys* from 'The Nutcracker' and the *Dance Of The Cygnets* from 'Swan Lake'.

The second half of the 19th century saw the emergence of several distinctly French composers, amongst them Jules Massenet (1842–1912), who significantly revitalized French opera. Included here is the beautiful *Méditation* from his opera 'Thaïs'.

Later that century, the Impressionist movement was in full swing in France, and Claude Debussy (1862–1918) is often thought to have been inspired by the painters of the time, appearing to emulate their style musically. Washes of sound, the use of scales and chords from other cultures, unusual orchestration and lavish use of the piano's sustaining pedal helped create new textures and colours. Included here is the evocative night piece *Clair de Lune*.

Writing at the same time as Debussy was Scott Joplin (1868-1917), the first black American to break into the white music market. His ragtime pieces for solo piano, so-called because of their syncopated 'ragged' rhythms, were irresistible, and his music became hugely popular. *The Entertainer* was immortalized in the 1970s film 'The Sting'.

Méditation
(from *Thaïs*)

Composed by Jules Massenet

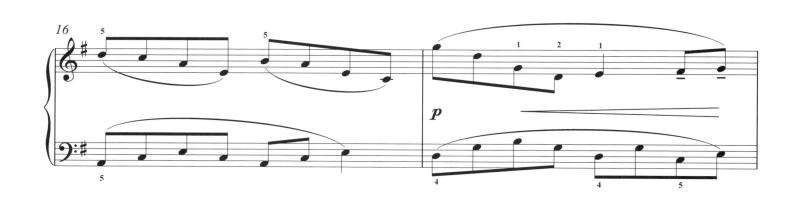

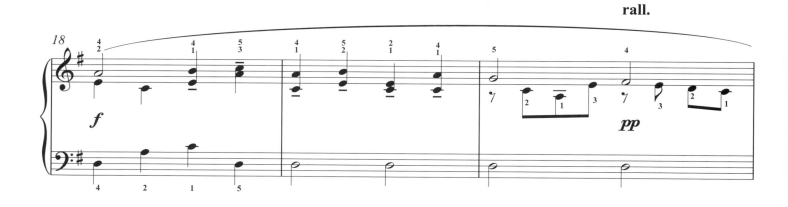

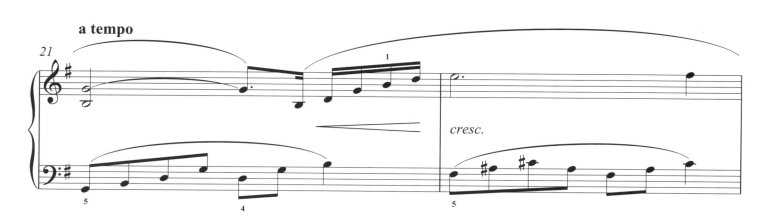

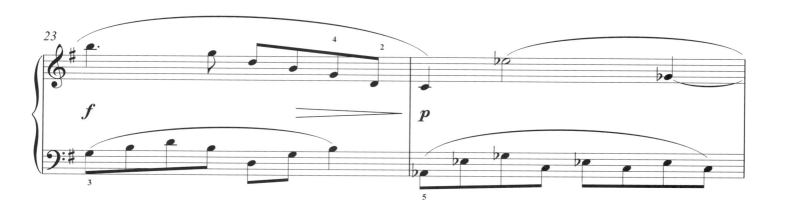

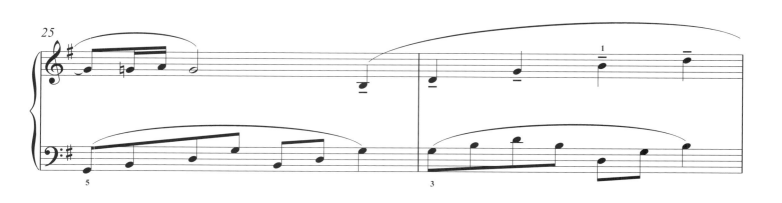

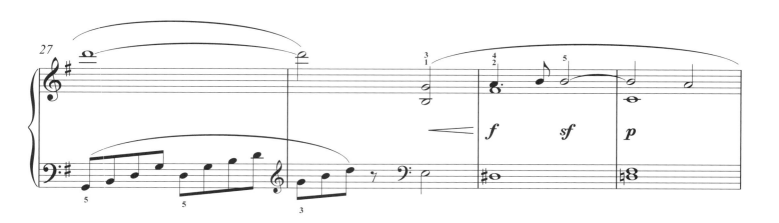

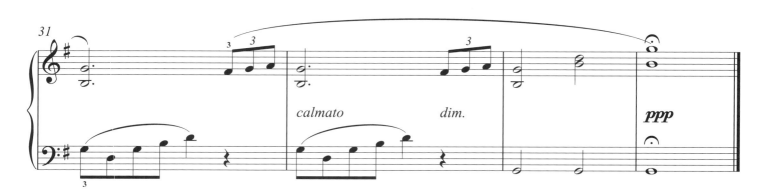

Air On The G String
(from Suite No.3 in D minor)

Composed by Johann Sebastian Bach

Lento, espressivo

Jesu, Joy Of Man's Desiring
(from Cantata 147)

Composed by Johann Sebastian Bach

Prélude No.1 in C major
(from *The Well-Tempered Clavier, Book 1*)

Composed by Johann Sebastian Bach

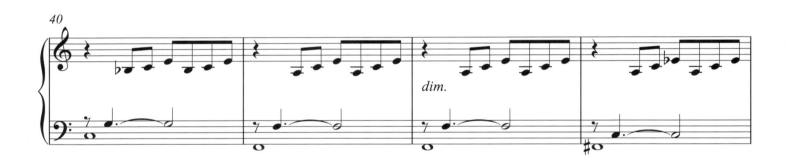

16

poco rit.

Bagatelle in G minor, Op.119, No.1

Composed by Ludwig van Beethoven

Allegretto

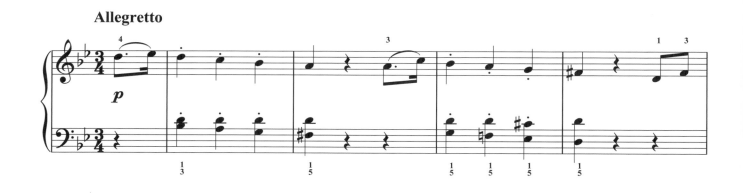

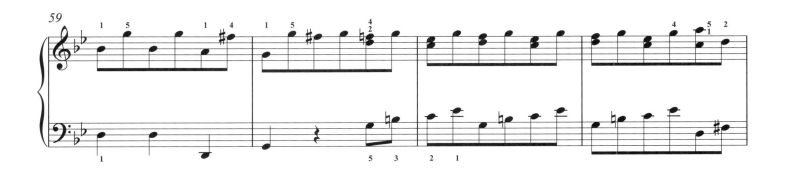

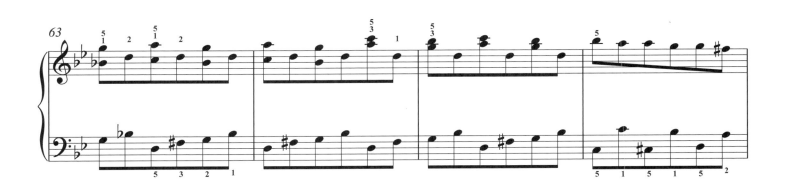

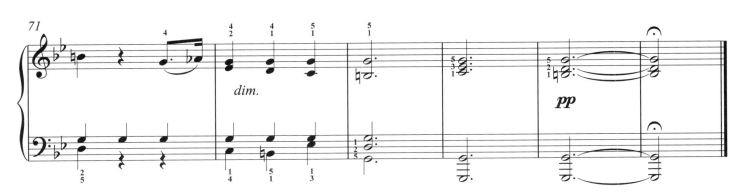

Sonata Pathètique, Op.13
(2nd movement)

Composed by Ludwig van Beethoven

Symphony No.5, Op.67
(1st movement)

Composed by Ludwig van Beethoven

Nocturne in E♭, Op.9, No.2

Composed by Frédéric Chopin

Prélude in C minor 'Funeral March'
Op.28, No.20

Composed by Frédéric Chopin

Prélude in E minor 'Suffocation'
Op.28, No.4

Composed by Frédéric Chopin

Clair de Lune
(from *Suite Bergamasque*)

Composed by Claude Debussy

Andante très expressif

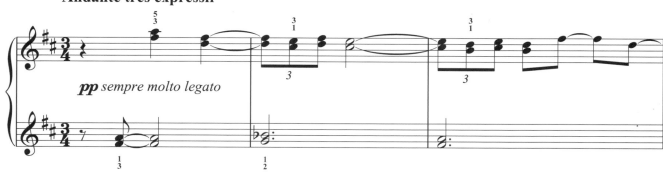

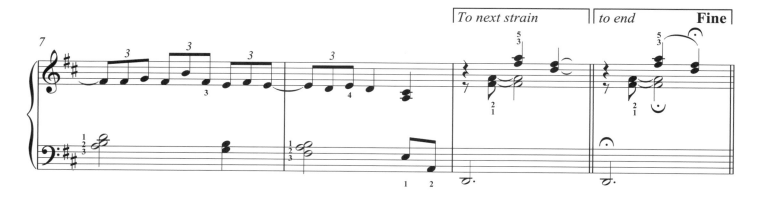

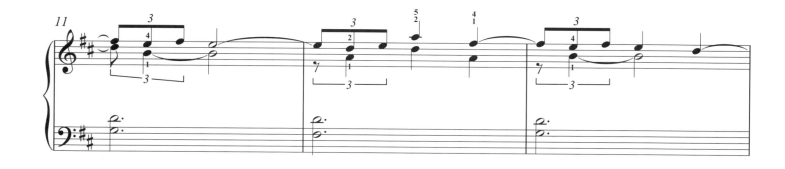

Air
(from *Water Music*)

Composed by George Frideric Handel

Largo

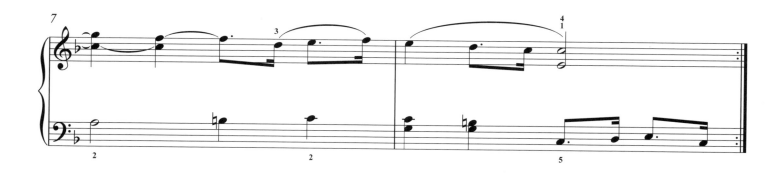

molto rit.

Sarabande in D minor

Composed by George Frideric Handel

Zadok The Priest
(*Coronation Anthem*)

Composed by George Frideric Handel

Andante maestoso

mp sempre cresc.

The Entertainer

Composed by Scott Joplin

Not Fast

to Coda ⊕

O, For The Wings Of A Dove
(from *Hear My Prayer*)

Composed by Felix Mendelssohn

Träumerei
(from *Kinderszenen*, Op.15, No.7)

Composed by Robert Schumann

cresc.

rit.　　a tempo

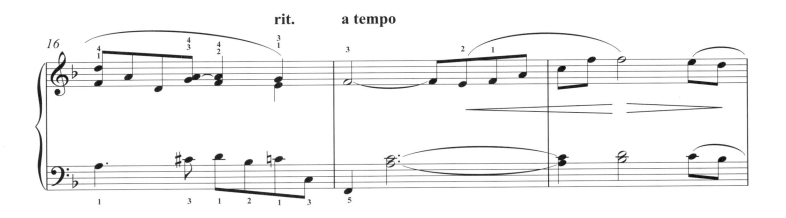

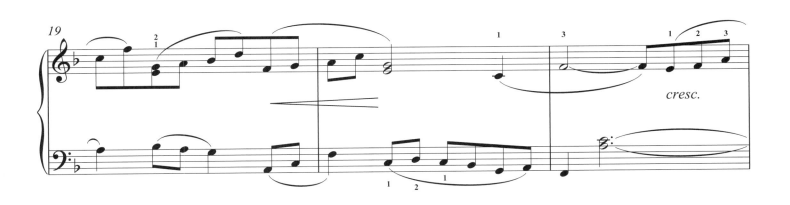

cresc.

rit.

p

Lacrimosa
(from *Requiem* K626)

Composed by Wolfgang Amadeus Mozart

Ave Verum Corpus, K618

Composed by Wolfgang Amadeus Mozart

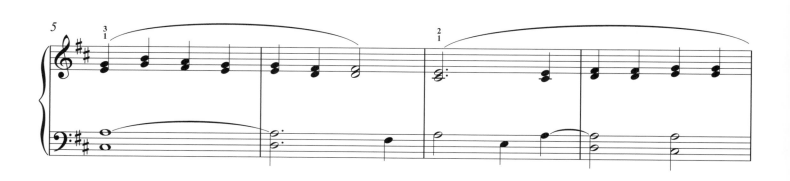

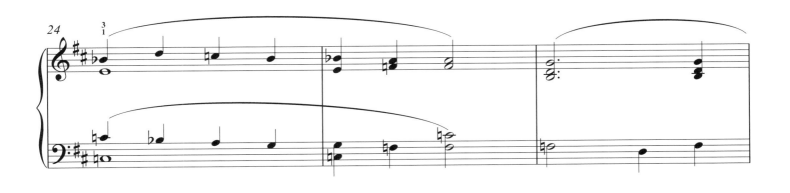

Ave Maria

Composed by Franz Schubert

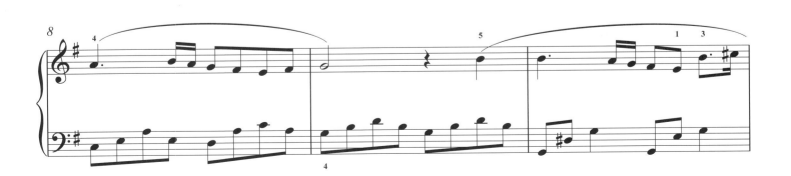

Trout Quintet, Op.114
(4th movement)

Composed by Franz Schubert

Dance Of The Cygnets
(from *Swan Lake*)

Composed by Pyotr Ilyich Tchaikovsky

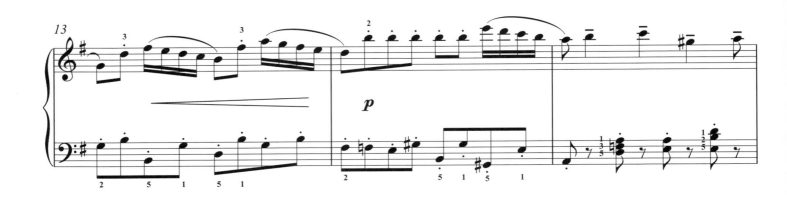

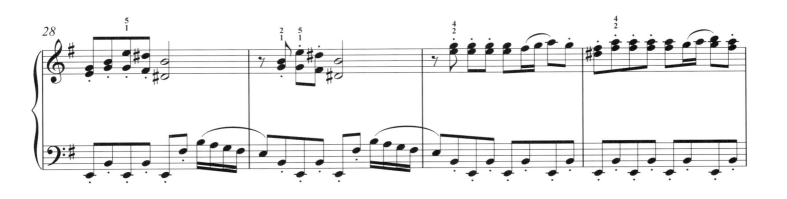

March Of The Toys
(from *The Nutcracker*)

Composed by Pyotr Ilyich Tchaikovsky

Tempo di marcia